Steam to Mallaig

Published by Famedram Publishers Limited, PO Box 3, Ellon, AB41 9EA
www.northernbooks.co.uk
Print: Imprint Digital

Cover: On the long climb from Loch nan Uamh to Beasdale

Steam to Mallaig

**Highlights
of the spectacular
Fort William-
Mallaig rail route**

Northern Books
from Famedram

Ready for the off from Fort William station.

FW
42

61994

BRITISH RAILWAYS

**Start of a memorable journey
to the Atlantic – at Mallaig**

Crossing the Nevis Bridge, with
Glen Nevis behind.

Swing bridge over the Caledonian
Canal at Banavie.

Locheil Outward Bound station,
with Ben Nevis behind

Nearing the end of the long climb
to the mighty Glenfinnan viaduct

Crossing the massive concrete
spans of the Glenfinnan viaduct

Twenty one arched spans of 15m (51ft) carry the line across the 380m (1250ft) Glenfinnan viaduct at a height of 30m (100ft).

Rare evening Glenfinnan crossing, just after the introduction of twice-a-day steam excursions.

Glenfinnan at last! The end of the long haul to Glenfinnan Station is in sight.

Glenfinnan – first stop on the route and home of the Glenfinnan Station Museum

Historic passing scenes at Glenfinnan as one Jacobite (actually a Waverley) bound for Mallaig meets another returning to Fort William

Still climbing from Glenfinnan towards the summit and the half way mark on the 40 mile journey to Mallaig.

After running alongside the road for a while the line heads into the hills once more and prepares for the long descent to the sea.

First brief glimpse of the sea – at Loch Ailort – just after passing the station of the same name (or nearly) – Lochailort.

First sight of the Atlantic proper, as the line crosses the Loch nan Uamh viaduct – eight 15m (51ft) arches – then enters a tunnel to start the long climb to the Beasdale bank.

Made it! The morning Jacobite reaches Beasdale after the long haul from the sea.

Gathering speed after the ascent of the 1 in 48 incline, Beasdale station is passed.

Rare late evening Jacobite excursion exits
the 320m (1050 ft.) Borrodale tunnel on
to the soaring Borrodale Bridge.

Caught in the evening sun, the massive main arch of the concrete Borrodale Bridge, a record breaking 39m (127ft) when built by 'Concrete Bob' McAlpine.

Nearing journey's end, the line approaches Morar, last station but one. Top left can be seen the peaks of the Isle of Rum, accessible by the Small Isles ferry service from Mallaig.

Morar, here we come. The Jacobite nears
the end of its journey.

Bells ring, lights flash – and a blast on the hooter for good measure for the Morar level crossing.

THE
WAVERLE

44871

26
D
SC

KEEP
OSSING
CLEAR

NTACT RAILWAY
phone
William 707703
STD 01397)

orar crossing

**Afternoon excursion train at the Morar
level crossing, once operated by the guard.**

Morar, and the silver sands in the background, as the final summit is climbed before the descent towards Mallaig.

Downhill all the way towards Glasnacardoch and the open sea, and Skye beyond.

Next stop Mallaig – with the Cuillins of Skye in the background.

The end of the line – some 40 miles after leaving Fort William, the afternoon departure reaches Mallaig.

Homeward bound – the setting sun catches a rare late evening Jacobite excursion crossing the Morar viaduct on its way back to Fort William close to 9pm at night.